An Easy Introduction to Cryptography

MUSTAFA ZIA

DEDICATION

For everybody who inspired me along the way,
For Mum, Zum and Q

CONTENTS

1 History 1

2 Commonly 6
Used Terms

3 Encryption 9
Methods

4 Affine 17
Substitutions

5 Making a 22
Substitution
Cipher Safer

6 Number 24
Theory

7 Stream 29
Ciphers

8 Key 34
Generation
and One Time
Pads

9 Public Key 41
Cryptography

1 HISTORY

<u>CRYPTOGRAPHY</u> : The origins of the word are Greek;

- "**kryptós**" meaning **secret** or **hidden**

- "**graphein**" meaning **writing**

Cryptography is the craft of protecting transmitted information from third party interception or tampering.

Cryptanalysis is the art of breaking such **ciphers** and understanding the hidden information. It has been around for thousands of years in one form or another, some of the earliest known examples of it are hieroglyphs from the time of the first kingdom of Egypt circa 1900BC, found on statues and monuments. This is not cryptography in the truest sense of the word, it is more so an example of another related art form;

Steaganography, which is simply **concealing** the message so that it cannot be found, and thus cannot be intercepted, understood, or tampered with. The "Father of History", Herodotus (484-425BC), tells us

1

of other ancient methods such as secret messages physically concealed beneath wax on wooden tablets or even tattoos on a slave's head concealed by regrown hair!

(A more recent proposal is that of applying Steaganography to DNA. The theory here is that a strand of DNA can be thought of a sequence of 4 letters- namely the bases **A**denine, **T**hymine, **G**uanine and **C**ytosine. Since the development of genetic sequencing, it is- in theory- easy to "edit" a strand of DNA i.e. encode the message in this four-letter alphabet and insert this sequence into a DNA strand. A small amount of DNA can then be concealed in a letter, postcard or even carried on your person!)

It is widely believed that modern cryptography originated originated amongst the Arabs, who were the first to document the methods of cryptanalysis. It was in fact the Arab mathematician Al-Kindi who is credited with the invention of the frequency analysis technique for breaking (mono alphabetic) substitution ciphers, sometime around AD800.

Essentially all ciphers remained vulnerable to the technique of frequency analysis until the development of the poly alphabetic cipher, and many remained so even afterwards. This changed when a practical poly alphabetic system was invented. It's method was originally described by Giovan Battista Bellaso in 1553. However, the scheme was later misattributed to Blaise de Vigenère in the 19th century, and is now widely known as the "Vigenère cipher" (which we will briefly touch on later.)

Cryptographic techniques were also rapidly proliferated during and after the time of the Renaissance due to the use by the Roman Catholic Church and citizens of the

Papal States. These were ciphers were regularly broken. This enthusiasm seems to be inherent in cryptography, for it was then - and remains today - intrinsically difficult to accurately assess how vulnerable one's cipher system actually is.

Although cryptography has a long and complex history, it wasn't until the 19th century that it developed to be something other than improvised approaches to either encryption or to finding weaknesses in crypto systems. During World War I the Admiralty broke German naval codes and played an important part in several naval engagements during the war, notably in detecting major German sorties into the North Sea. that led to the British fleet being sent out to intercept them. However its most important contribution was probably in decrypting the Zimmermann Telegram, a cable from the German Foreign Office sent via Washington to ambassador Heinrich von Eckardt in Mexico which resulted in bringing the United States into the war.

In 1917, Gilbert Vernam devised a teleprinter cipher in which a preprepared key, kept on paper tape, is combined, character by character with the plaintext message to produce the ciphertext. This led to the development of devices as cipher machines, and to the only unbreakable cipher, the One Time Pad. Claude Shannon, "the father of mathematical cryptography" proved this.

By World War II, mechanical and electromechanical cipher machines were in wide use, although manual systems also continued in use. Huge advances were made in both cipher design and cryptanalysis, all in secrecy. Information about this period has begun to be declassified as the official British 50-year secrecy period has came to an end and as US archives have slowly opened.

It is widely known that Germans made heavy use, in several variants, of an electromechanical rotor machine known as Enigma.

German code breaking during WW2 also had some success, most importantly by breaking the Naval Cipher No.3. This enabled them to track and sink Atlantic convoys. The German military also deployed several mechanical attempts at a one-time pad. The German Foreign Office began to use the one-time pad in 1919. These are just some historical examples of cryptography usage, which leads us onto modern day cryptography.

Encryption in modern times is achieved by using algorithms that have a key to encrypt and decrypt information. These keys convert the messages and data into "gibberish" through encryption and then return them to the original form through decryption. In general, the longer the key is, the more difficult it is to crack the code. This holds true because deciphering an encrypted message by "brute force" would require the attacker to try every possible key. To put this into context, an 8-bit key would have 2^8 or 256 possible keys. A 56-bit key would have 72 quadrillion or 2^{56} possible keys to try and decipher the message. In general, with a key of length n bits, there are 2^n possible keys.

Most secure internet traffic is at least 128-bit encrypted (although 256 bit encryption is also becoming more common) which gives near enough 2^{128} possible keys (or in words three hundred forty undecillion, two hundred eighty-two decillion, three hundred sixty-six nonillion, nine hundred twenty octillion, nine hundred thirty-eight septillion, four hundred sixty-three sextillion, four hundred sixty-three quintillion, three hundred seventy-four quadrillion, six hundred seven trillion, four hundred thirty-one billion, seven hundred sixty-eight million, two hundred eleven thousand, four hundred fifty-six- which is a number completely beyond comprehension!)

The large number of operations (2^{128}) required to try all possible 128-bit keys is widely considered impractical (because it would simply take too long) for conventional computing techniques for the foreseeable future. However, experts theorise new computing technologies that may have processing power superior to current computer technology. (If a quantum computer capable of running Shor's or Grover's algorithm was invented, it would theoretically be possible to crack 128bit encryption relatively easily. But this is beyond the scope of this text.)

With modern advances in computing and processing power, these numbers are becoming easier to decipher; however, as technology advances, so does the quality of encryption. Since WW2, one of the most notable advances in the study of cryptography is the introduction of the public-key. These are algorithms that use a public key to encrypt, but a particular, private key to decrypt.

There have been some significant cracking of deployed crypto-systems in recent years. Notable examples of such fractured ciphers include the first Wi-Fi encryption scheme WEP, the Content Scrambling System used for encrypting DVD use, some early ciphers used in GSM cell phones, and the cipher used in the widely deployed MIFARE smart cards (used in Oyster cards and the like).

2 COMMONLY USED TERMS

Alice and **Bob** are two commonly used place holder names. The names are used for convenience; for example, "Alice sends a message to Bob encrypted with his public key" is easier to follow than "Party A sends a message to Party B encrypted using Party B's public key." Following the alphabet, these specific names have become common in these fields—helping somewhat technical topics to be explained in a more understandable fashion.

Alice and Bob could be on-line businesses or friends trying to have a private conversation. They can't stop Eve listening to their radio signals (or tapping their phone line), so what can they do to keep their communication secret? (This is what we will try and gain an understanding of!)

Eve is considered to be the nemesis of Alice and Bob. This is who is trying to intercept or change the message. We generally assume that Eve can view the encrypted message.

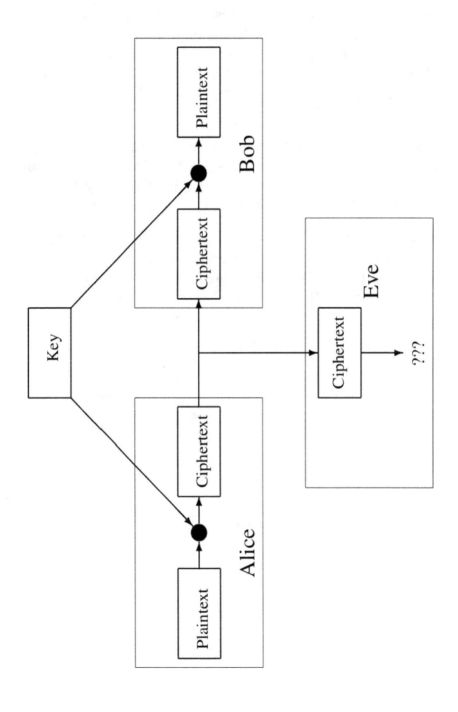

Plaintext: The plaintext is not quite the same as the message being sent. The message has to be translated into some standard form to be encrypted; this could be leaving out the punctuation or turning it into a sequence of numbers. There is nothing secret about the plaintext; knowing the plaintext is equivalent to knowing the message.

Ciphertext: The ciphertext is what is actually transmitted. Alice and Bob assume that Eve can intercept the ciphertext so they must design the cipher (system) so that she will not be able to recover the plaintext.

Key: The encryption uses some extra information, known as the key, which may be varied from one transmission to another. Both Alice and Bob must have information about the key in order to encrypt and decrypt the ciphertext.

3 ENCRYPTION METHODS

As far as basic encryption methods are concerned there are three types that we shall concern ourselves with:

Substitution: Individual letters are replaced by different letters in a systematic way.

(It is possible to allow a letter to 'replaced' by itself.) This may be more complicated than just a single permutation; we may apply different permutations to the letters in different positions.

The key is the sequence of permutations that we applied.

Transposition: The order of the letters in the plaintext is rearranged in a predefined and systematic way. **The key is the permutation that is applied to the letters.**

Codebook: This is similar to the substitution cipher (above) with an important difference- we replace entire words with words of completely different meanings.

The key is the codebook; the list of words and their replacements.

(For our purposes, a "code" replaces certain key words in the message by other words or combinations of symbols, as defined in the code book. This is in contrast with a cipher, which defines itself on the individual letters or symbols.)

Pig Latin is a simple form of *transposition cipher* with a "null" character. A few examples are;

cat → atcay

dog → ogday

simply → implysay

is → isyay

apple → appleyay

octopus → octopusyay

rhythm → rhythmay

A quick internet search on "Pig Latin" will garner many more useful rules and examples than I can include here, but the above examples should offer somewhat of an insight as to what is going on.

Substitution Ciphers

One of the simplest (mono alphabetic) substitution ciphers is when we take a permutation of the alphabet in which the plaintext is written, and substitute each symbol by its image under the permutation.

The key to the cipher is the permutation used; anyone possessing this can easily apply the inverse permutation to recover the plaintext.

If we take a piece or ordinary English text, ignore spaces and punctuation, and convert all letters to capitals, then the alphabet consists of 26 symbols, and so the number of keys is ;

$$26! = 403291461126605635584000000.$$

This is a large enough number to discourage anyone making a complete list of all possible keys. However, the cipher is usually very easy to break.

A permutation can be represented by writing down the letters of the alphabet in the usual order, and writing its image underneath each letter. To find the inverse, write the bottom row above the top row, and then sort the columns so that the new top row is in its natural order. An illustrative example is;

The inverse of the permutation:

A B C D E F G H I J K L M N O P Q R S T U V W X Y Z

T H E Q U I C K B R O W N F X J M P S V L A Z Y D G

is

A B C D E F G H I J K L M N O P Q R S T U V W X Y Z

V I G Y C N Z B F P H U Q M K R D J S A E T L O X W

Caesar Shift

A fundamental substitution cipher is the Caesar Shift (named for it's use by Julius Caesar himself!) Each letter is shifted a fixed number of places to the right. (Caesar allegedly used a shift of three places. He also, of course, used the Latin alphabet- but we'll stick with English!) We regard the alphabet as cyclical, so that the letter following Z is A.

Thus, for example, the table below shows a right shift of 6 places:

A B C D E F G H I J K L M N O P Q R S T U V W X Y Z

G H I J K L M N O P Q R S T U V W X Y Z A B C D E F

The message "All hail Caesar" would be enciphered by as "Grr ngor Igkygx". The key is simply the

number of places that the letters are shifted (in our case 6), and the cipher is decrypted by applying

the shift in the opposite direction (6 places back). To make it slightly harder to break, we would capitalise all letters in the ciphertext; thus eliminating any obvious names of places, people etc. Our example above would become "GRRN GORI GKYG XXXX". You will notice that we have used a standard blocks of 4 letters then a space, we have also filled the last block with "padding" in the form of the last three letters.

The Caesar cipher is not difficult to break. There are only 26 possible keys, and we can try them all until one eventually makes sense. Certainly one of the 26 attempts will make sense, and it is easy to

break it into words and discard the padding. There are other tricks that can be used; in English text, the most common letter is usually E. If we can spot these patterns, then we can make a n attempt to guess the correct shift. Our example is too short to show much- if any- statistical regularity, but with longer text it is certainly possible.

Frequencies of Letters

Words are not random combinations of symbols so they will show various statistical regularities and patterns. For example, in English, the most common letter is E; in a typical (not too short) piece

of English, approximately 12% of all the letters will be E.

Note that even for English text the numbers vary although not too much. They are usually in order most regular appearance; E, T, A, O, I.

However, in other languages the order is quite different. For example, in German, the order is typically E, N, I, R, S.

As a interesting side note, in 1939, Ernest Vincent Wright wrote a novel called "Gadsby". The novel was written as a lipogram and does not include words that contain the letter "e"! That's 50,110 words without the letter "e". Quite an impressive feat, and a surefire way to disrupt any frequency analysis!

We can also analyse trigrams, or longer sequences, among the most common trigrams in English are THE, ING, THA, AND, ION.

Breaking any cipher is an art; it cannot be done by applying a formula. But there are some rules to follow when doing attempting to break a Caesar Shift. Part of the ciphertext is;

RZOLB	QJOWW	QBWIR	DQFQE	VICOB	OKOLR	UVIDW	IVTOH
OVZMA	UFUIR	UVEWM	DWOBH	UOVYO	RQRZO	UBWRM	RZOSZ
ITRQW	COIBQ	DOTUO	VYORQ	RZOWR	MTOVR	BOYRQ	RQRZO
WRMTO	VRAIT	OWRIR	MROWC	ZUYZD	QBOHO	BSZIB	BWIVT
ARZOL	BQJOW	WQBCI	WJUVO	TUJZO	DOEIV	ZUWRO	TFSML
MROFI	ROQBY	QVRUV	MOTIA	UVMRO	FQVEO	BRZIV	QVRZO
AOIVT	WZQMF	TRZUW	ZILLO	VRZOW	RMTOV	RWCZQ	EIAUV
IHORZ	OFOYR	MBOBQ	QAUAA	OTUIR	OFSCO	BORZO	XOTRU
OTUVI	TTURU	QVRZO	LBQJO	WWQBC	IWJUV	OTUJZ	TRQFO
LFIUV	UVEIT	UJJUY	MFRLI	WWIEO	QBUJZ	OJIUF	OWJUV
QMEZR	ZOWSF	FIDMW	ZOCIW	JUVOT	UJZOF	OJRRZ	KOTOX
ISCUR	ZQMRR	ZOBOY	RQBWL	OBAUW	WUQVI	VTUJZ	ORRZB
WIFFQ	COTQV	FSQVO	TISQJ	JJQBR	ZOLMB	LQWOR	JQBIT
RWLIB	RRQQK	IZIVT	UVYQV	RBQFF	UVERZ	OLBQJ	UOTCI
ZOSCO	BOJQB	YOTRQ	RIKOI	VQIRZ	VQRRQ	FOIHO	ZOYUR
OIBYZ	QJAQB	OFMYB	IRUHO	QBFOW	WQVOB	QMWLQ	SJQBU
							WIVTR
							VIUVW
							WRWXX

We first count the frequencies of the letters. The most common of the 715 letters with their frequencies, are given below:

O   R   Q   I   U   W   V   B   Z

99 72 59 50 49 48 45 43 43

We also notice that RZ is a very common digram, with 23 occurrences. So we might guess the following identifications: O = e, R = t and Z = h. This gives:

```
theLB QJeWW QBWIt DQFQE VICeB eKeLt UVIDW QFMte IVTeH
eVhMA UFUIt UVEWM DWeBH UeVYe tQthe UBWtM TeVtW theSh
ITtQW CeIBQ DeTUe VYetQ theWt MTeVt BeYtQ BWIVT tQthe
WtMTe VtAIT eWtIt MteWC hUYhD QBeHe BShIB TFSML QVthe
AtheL BQJeW WQBCI WJUVe TUJhe DeEIV hUWte IYhUV EIAUV
MteFI teQBY QVtUV MeTIA UVMte FQVEe BthIV theJU XeTtU
```

The other common letters probably include a, i, o and n. There are various clues that help us to make the correct assumptions. For example, looking at the string "*tQthe*", which occurs several times. Here, *the* is probably either a word or the beginning of a word like *then*. If this is right, *tQ* ends a word, and the most likely possibility is that *Q* = *o*.

Another clue is that *WW* occurs many times in the text. Double letters are not very common in English other than; *ee, ll* and *ss* are the most common, so probably *W* = *s*. After a certain amount of guesswork of this sort, we begin to recognise more complicated words, and we find eventually that the substitution is:

```
a b c d e f g h i j k l m n o p q r s t u v w x y z
I D Y T O J E Z U P K F A V Q L G B W R M H C X S N
```

and the message is :

"The professors at Bologna were kept in absolute and even humiliating subservience to their students. They had to swear obedience to the student rectors and to the student made statutes, which bore very hardly upon them. The professor was fined if he began his teaching a minute late or continued a..."

4 AFFINE SUBSTITUTIONS

These are a special subclass of substitution ciphers. The substitution used above is especially interesting- It maps a to I, b to D, c to Y, and so on;

increasing the plaintext letter by 1 place moves the ciphertext letter back 5 places (or forward 21 places). In other words, if the letters of the alphabet are numbered from 0 to 25, so that a is represented by 0, b by 1, . . . , z by 25, then the substitution takes the form :

$$x \rightarrow 21x + 8 \ (\text{mod } 26)$$

Such a substitution and the cipher that is produced is called *affine.*

(At the end of the book we will find a short piece about modular arithmetic, for those of us who need reminding!)

The Caesar shift is a special case of an affine cipher, having the form :

$$x \rightarrow x + b \ (\text{mod } 26)$$

for some fixed b. The general form of an affine cipher is :

$$x \rightarrow ax + b \pmod{26}$$

for some fixed a and b, with the caveat that this map be invertible. The advantage is that the key is simple! Instead of needing a general permutation of the letters, we only need to remember the numbers a and b mod 26. An interesting and important question is;

"What affine ciphers are possible and how can they be inverted?"

To answer this we must first decide when an affine substitution is a permutation, and apply the following theorem (we will not go into the details of how this is derived).

Theorem: The affine map $x \rightarrow ax + b$ is a permutation if and only if $gcd(a, n) = 1$.

Write $\theta_{a,b}$ for the map $x \rightarrow ax + b \pmod{n}$, where $gcd(a, n) = 1$

If we compose two such maps then their composition is also affine. The identity permutation $x \rightarrow x$ is the map $\theta_{1,0}$. So to find the inverse of $\theta_{a,b}$ in the form $\theta_{a',b'}$ we have to solve the congruences ;

$$aa' \equiv 1 \qquad \pmod{n}$$

$$ba' + b' \equiv 0 \pmod{n}$$

The first congruence has a unique solution mod n, which can be found by Euclid's Algorithm. Then the second congruence also has a unique solution, namely $b' \equiv -ba'$ (mod n). (Of course, we can write a' as a^{-1} , and then $b' = -ba^{-1}$ (but this is not usually b^{-1} and may not even exist). In particular, when n = 26, we want to invert the map $\theta_{21,8}$. By trial and error (or by the use of Euclid's Algorithm); $21 \cdot 5 \equiv 1 \pmod{26}$; and then $-5 \cdot 8 \equiv 12$

(mod 26). So the inverse of $\theta_{21,8}$ is $\theta_{5,12}$.

We must now define *Euler's Totient Function* and some important *Theorems:*

Euler's totient function φ is the function on the positive integers given by

φ (n) = {number of congruence classes a mod n such that gcd(a, n) = 1}

We give a formula for it later.

Theorem: If we let $n = p_1{}^{a_1}p_2{}^{a_2} \cdots p_r{}^{a_r}$, where p_1 , $p_2 , \ldots , p_r$ are distinct primes

and $a_1 , a_2 , \ldots , a_r > 0$.

Then ,

$\varphi (n) = p_1{}^{a_1 -1} (p_1 - 1) \, p_2{}^{a_2 -1} (p_2 - 1) \cdots p_r{}^{a_r -1} (p_r - 1).$

Of course, $\varphi (1) = 1$.

For example, $26 = 2 \cdot 13$, so $\varphi (26) = 1 \cdot 12 = 12$. The congruence classes coprime to 26 are represented by the odd numbers from 1 to 25 excluding 13.

Theorem: The set of affine permutations mod n is a group of order $n \cdot \varphi (n)$

There are therefore $26 \cdot 12 = 312$ affine permutations! If we know or suspect that a substitution cipher is affine we could try all 312 keys- although this is not trivial by hand. The method of looking for patterns of consecutive letters does not apply. Like any substitution cipher, an affine cipher is vulnerable to frequency analysis. Its advantage is the small size of the key (two numbers rather than a complete permutation).

An example for clarification:

To decrypt the following affine substitution cipher:

```
JZQOU DQGKZ UULYU MKUOX LQJQJ ZQZCW ZQDYU MDXUJ
QRJCE LQEDR CRWGL UUIEJ JZQEP QDEWQ QEDRC RWGCR
JZCGK ZEDJJ ZQYJQ LLJZQ GJUDY
```

We calculate the frequency distribution to be as follows:

C	D	E	G	I	J	K	L	M	O	P	Q	R	U	W	X	Y	Z
6	8	7	5	1	13	3	6	2	2	1	15	6	10	4	2	4	10

The most common letter Q in the given cipher is likely to be e. We also see that the trigram JZQ occurs five times and so is likely to be *"the"*. This gives J = t and Z = h. The letters Q and Z are x_{16} and x_{25} (where we have n = 26 letters here), while e and h are x_4 and x_7. Thus the parameters a and b satisfy

$$4a + b \equiv 16 \pmod{26}$$

$$7a + b \equiv 25 \pmod{26}$$

from which we find a = 3 and b = 4. Now we can compute the inverse of this affine transformation, (which will be the decryption map). If the inverse is i → a'i + b' , then we have (using the formula from) earlier:

$$3a' = 1, \text{ so } a' = 9;$$

$$4'a + b' = 0, \text{ so } b' = 16.$$

From this the entire substitution can be worked out- as an exercise try and decrypt the cipher above using the decryption map we just found.

It is quicker to solve directly for the decryption map $\theta_{c,d}$.

The equations, decoding "QZ" as "eh" are $16c + d \equiv 4$ (mod 26) and $25c + d \equiv 7$ (mod 26). The second equation minus the first is $9c \equiv 3$ (mod 26), thus $c \equiv 9$ (mod 26). From which we can easily deduce that $d \equiv 4 - 144 = -140 \equiv -10 \equiv 16$ (mod 26). Naturally we have $c = a'$ and $d = b'$ (mod 26).

5 MAKING A SUBSTITUTION CIPHER SAFER

A substitution cipher can be solved by frequency analysis, which makes it insecure for all but the shortest messages. However, there are some improvements that can be made. The first two rely on using a different alphabet for the ciphertext, with more characters than the plaintext alphabet. (For example we could use an alphabet of 100 characters, represented by symbols 00, 01, . . . , 99.).

Nulls: These are additional symbols in the cipher alphabet which do not have any meaning but are inserted in random positions to disrupt the frequency analysis. (It is also plausible to insert extraneous letters from the normal cipher alphabet, but you must consider how Bob will handle the decrypted result -where is the null symbol (if any) in bring tein soldiers?)

Homophones: We can translate the same letter in plaintext by several different letters in ciphertext. For example, if we use a 100-character cipher alphabet, we can associate about as many characters with each plaintext letter as its percentage frequency in normal text (say, 12 characters for e, 9 for t, and so on). Then we randomly decide which character to substitute for each occurrence of a letter. In the ciphertext, each character will occur approximately the same number of times. However, the ciphertext is still not random, and patterns of digraphs and trigraphs may be recognised.

Use of language: We can further disrupt the analysis by using words from other languages, or by careful exclusion of words or letters. As an example of what can be done, see, Gadsby, by Ernest Vincent Wright- as mentioned earlier. (The author allegedly tied down the E key of his typewriter to write the book.)

Another trick is to write words phonetically, or to use text messaging abbreviations. Examples include ("nite" instead of "night"), omit common vowels ("txt" instead of "text"), use of numerals 2, 4 and 8 instead of to, for and ate, and maybe even use of "emoticons" such as ;-) as a fundamental part of the text, would give a frequency analysis quite different from standard English!

Transposition: The substitution can be combined with transposition (which is simply permuting the order or position of the characters in the ciphertext in a specified way). This will help to destroy the patterns of digram and trigram frequencies. This is just an example, we can always combine the substitution cipher with any other cipher.

With these improvements, even a substitution cipher can be effective for a short message!

6 NUMBER THEORY

This is a quick reminder of some basic number theory which we will cement our understanding of what we have seen so far and far more importantly what is yet to be seen.

Modular Arithmetic:

In modular arithmetic, the numbers we deal with are only integers and the operations used are addition, subtraction, multiplication and division. The only difference between modular arithmetic and the "normal" arithmetic is that, in modular arithmetic all operations are performed with respect to a positive integer (i.e. the modulus). A familiar example is that of a clock face.

Two odd numbers are congruent modulo 2 because all odd numbers can be written as $2n+1$;

Two even numbers are congruent modulo 2 because all even numbers can be written as $2n+0$;

$38 \equiv 23 \bmod 15$ because $38 = 15*2 + 8$ and $23 = 15 + 8$;

-1 ≡ 1 mod 2 because -1 = -1*2+1 and 1 = 0*2+1;

8 ≡ 3 mod 5 because 8 = 5+3 and 3 = 0*5+3;

-8 ≡ 2 mod 5 because -8 = -2*5+2 and 2 = 0*5+2;

8 ≢ -8 mod 5 because 8 = 5+3 and -8 = -2*5+2.
The remainders 3 and 2 are not the same.

35*7 ≡ 245 ≡ 0 mod 5

-47*(5+1) ≡ -282 ≡ 3 mod 5

373^3≡ 50653 ≡ 3 mod 5

Congruence is an **Equivalence Relation:** If *a* and *b*are congruent modulo *n*, then they have no difference in modular arithmetic under modulo *n*. Because of this, in "mod *n*" arithmetic we usually use *n* numbers 0, 1, 2, ..., n-1. All the other numbers can be found congruent to one of the *n* numbers.

For division, it is not so simple because division is not defined for every number. This means that it is **not always possible to perform division in modular arithmetic**. Firstly, as in ordinary arithmetic, division by zero is not defined,so 0 cannot be the divisor. The interesting part is that the multiples of the modulus are congruent to 0. For example, 5, -5, 10, -10, ... are all congruent to 0 when the modulus is 5. So not only 4/0 is not allowed, 4/10 is also not allowed when the modulus is 5.

So when is modular division is defined?

When the **multiplicative inverse** (or inverse) of the divisor exists! The inverse of an integer *a* under modulus *n* is an integer *b* such that *a*b* ≡ 1 mod *n*. An integer can have either one or no inverse. The inverse of *a* can be another integer or *a* itself. For example, we can see that 1 (mod 6) has an inverse, which is itself and 5 also has an inverse which is also itself. But 2, 3 and 4 do not have inverses. Whether an integer has the inverse or not depends on the integer itself and also the modulus.

The rule is that the inverse of an integer a exists if and only if a and the modulus n are coprime. That is, the only positive integer which divides both a and n is 1. In particular, when n is prime, then every integer except 0 and the multiples of n is coprime to n, so every number except 0 has a corresponding inverse under modulo n. Most of the time it is not easy to determine when 2 integers are coprime. For example, are 225 and 157 coprime? This is not immediately obvious or intuitive. Fortunately we can use the Euclidean Algorithm to find out! The Euclidean Algorithm is how we can find out what is called the greatest common divisor (or **gcd**) of 2 positive integers. If the gcd of two integers is 1, they are clearly coprime.

For example:

Find **gcd(225,157)**.

Here is the calculation:

$$225 = 157 \cdot 1 + 68$$

$$157 = 68 \cdot 2 + 21$$

$$68 = 21 \cdot 3 + 5$$

$$21 = 5 \cdot 4 + 1$$

$$5 = 1 \cdot 5 + 0$$

So **gcd(225,157) = 1**.

Thus **225 and 157 ARE coprime**!

The Euclidean algorithm also finds integers **u** and **v** such that gcd(a,b) = ua+vb. In the above example, we can work back up the chain:

$$1 = 21 - 5 \cdot 4$$

$$= 21 - (68 - 21 \cdot 3) \cdot 4 = 21 \cdot 13 - 68 \cdot 4$$

$$= (157 - 68 \cdot 2) \cdot 13 - 68 \cdot 4 = 157 \cdot 13 - 68 \cdot 30$$

$$= 157 \cdot 13 - (225 - 157) \cdot 30 = 157 \cdot 43 - 225 \cdot 30.$$

So we have **u = −30, v = 43**

This last step is how we can find inverses mod n. For example, gcd(21, 26) = 1, and Euclid's algorithm shows that $1 = (-4) \cdot 26 + 5 \cdot 21$; so $5 \cdot 21 \equiv 1 \pmod{26}$, and the inverse of 21 (mod 26) is 5.

If you would like to extend this idea do research the "Chinese Remainder Theorem". It has a wonderful proof and it helps to answer problems such as:

(Taken from the 4th century text Sun Tsu Suan Ching (Master Sun's Arithmetic Manual):

There is an unknown number of objects. When counted in threes, the remainder is 2; when counted in fives, the remainder is 3; when counted in sevens, the remainder is 2. How many objects are there?

The problem asks for an integer N such that $N \equiv 2 \pmod 3$, $N \equiv 3 \pmod 5$, and $N \equiv 2 \pmod 7$. One solution is given as

$$N = 2 \cdot 70 + 3 \cdot 21 + 2 \cdot 15 = 233.$$

It is clear that adding or subtracting a multiple of 105 from any solution gives another solution; so the smallest solution is

$$N = 233 - 2 \cdot 105 = 23$$

The answer is given in prose:

Not in every third person is there one aged three score and ten,

On five plum trees only twenty-one boughs remain,

The seven learned men meet every fifteen days,

We get our answer by subtracting one hundred and five over and over again.

7 STREAM CIPHERS

The fundamental idea of a Stream Cipher is to use different substitutions for different letters of the plaintext. An important principle that must be assumed is **Kerckhoff's Principle.**

This states that:

"A cryptosystem should be secure even if everything about the system, except the key, is public knowledge." Claude Shannon also independently reformulated this as *"the enemy knows the system".*

Shannon's maxim states this as:

"One ought to design systems under the assumption that the enemy will immediately gain full familiarity with them".

This methodology is widely embraced by modern cryptographers, very much in contrast to the previous "security through obscurity" approach- a common analogy likens it to leaving the rear door of a house open because a potential burglar might not see it!

To clarify, **Alice and Bob must always assume that Eve knows the encryption system they are using, as well as having intercepted the ciphertext. All they can hope to keep secret is the key.** This is because, although cryptographers are always inventing new methods and systems, knowledge of these systems will soon spread within the intelligence community.

The Vigenère Cipher:

The idea here is simply a cipher in which a different Caesar shift is applied to each letter of the plaintext.

An example:

Let's shift the first letter by 5, the second by 14, the third by 23, the fourth by 4, and the fifth by 18. Thus the word *"enemy"* would be encrypted as *"JBBQQ"*. Note that the two occurrences of "e" in the original message are replaced by different letters (J and B). Different letters in the plaintext become the same in the ciphertext. The key to this cipher is the sequence (5, 14, 23, 4, 18). Instead of having to remember the sequence of numbers, it is much more practical to remember the letters or words obtained by shifting the letter "a" by these numbers. In our example, aaaaa would become FOXES; which is the key to the cipher!

An example:

e	n	e	m	y	p	a	t	r	o	l	s
F	O	X	E	S	F	O	X	E	S	F	O
J	B	B	Q	Q	U	O	Q	V	G	Q	G

So:

The ciphertext is JBBQQ UOQVG QG.

The key is a simple word or phrase that is easily memorised and can be changed frequently.

Breaking the Vigenère Cipher:

The Vigenère cipher was an amazing advance on the mono alphabetic substitution cipher used for many years. There are 2 major weaknesses, which eventually led to a cryptanalysis technique for it:

- The cipher applied to each letter is a simple Caesar shift, which is very easy to break

and

- The key string repeats after a relatively short number of steps.

If we know that the keyword contains 5 letters. Then we can divide the ciphertext into 5 segments or **strings.**

- The 1st string will contain the 1st, 6th, 11th, ... , letter.

- The 2nd string will contain the 2nd, 7th, 12th, ... , letter.

- ... and so on and so forth...

Each string is now a Caesar cipher and can be attacked by the methods already discussed. (Digram/ Trigram frequency analysis won't work since letters that are consecutive in one of the sub strings were originally 5 steps apart in the message.) The letter frequency and more importantly the frequency patterns of consecutive in the alphabet CAN be applied. Once we have an approximate decryption of an individual string, the strings are simply reassembled to give the message!

The question that you should now be asking is "How do we determine the length of the key?"

Trial and error could be used, although the frequency analysis is not likely to give useful answers unless the assumed length is a small multiple of the true length!

A much better method uses the repetition in the ciphertext. This is known as **Kasiski's method:**

- First, guess the keyword length m, by finding the greatest common divisor of the distance apart of the most common digrams or trigrams.

- Then divide the message into sub strings each consisting of the letters congruent to i mod m for i = 1, 2, . . . , m, and apply frequency analysis to determine the shift associated with each sub string.

Strengthening the Vigenère Cipher:

The cryptographers now had two tasks:

1. They had to find a way of producing a non-repeating key;

2. To make the frequency analysis more difficult, they had to use an arbitrary permutation of the alphabet in each position, as opposed to a shift.

These additional requirements make it much more

difficult to use the ciphers quickly especially

battlefield situations. So it was necessary to move from hand to machine for the encryption and decryption.

One important tip when using the Vigenère cipher, is to apply is more than once using different keys! In doing so one makes it significantly more difficult to perform the cryptanalysis. An important rule to remember is that the Lowest Common Multiple (**lcm**) of the length of the keys applied to the same piece of text is equivalent to using a key of that length! (This directly addresses the first problem). So, for example if we used keys: *"strong"*, *"independent"*, "cryptographer" then the lcm(6,11,13) = 6*11*13 = 858. So in practice we have just used a key with length 858, this is useful for a long message of length approaching 858. We need to be careful to choose keys whose lengths have no common factors, otherwise this will reduce our key length.

8

KEY GENERATION AND ONE TIME PADS

Ideally, the very best keys are a completely random sequence of letters from the alphabet. Known as a "One Time Pad". This provides an absolutely secure form of encryption, mathematically proved to be unbreakable!! In practice however, it is very difficult to generate a truly random sequence. It is highly likely that one time pads were produced and used by the intelligence communities, especially during the Cold War. Rumours of the CIA employing people to record coin flips to generate "random" sequences exist!

How do we tell if a sequence is random?

By definition, 'random' means 'selected from the set of all possible sequences, any sequence being equally likely' But this definition refers to the set of all possible sequences, and doesn't tell us anything about a single sequence. Any sequence can occur, even a constant sequence! A completely different definition was proposed by Kolmogorov, who said:

"A sequence is random if it cannot be generated by an algorithm with a short description that is much shorter than the sequence itself"

Using this definition the string of digits of π, is not random!

One time pads are best used when the "random" key has the same length as the the plaintext (we attempted to replicate this by repeated use of the Vigenère cipher- with varying key lengths above).

Key Distribution:

One weakness of all the ciphers we have studied so far is the problem of key distribution. If Eve can get hold of the key, then she can decrypt the cipher. On the other hand, Alice and Bob must both know the key, or they cannot communicate. So they must share the key by some secure method which Eve cannot infiltrate.

One classical method that must have been used is to give a spy the key (which may be one copy of the one time pad, the other copy being retained by the issuing authority) then send her into the field. Considering the key must never be reused, she can only send back as much information as the key she possesses. She must then return to base for a new one time pad. This is a plausible method, assuming the spy keeps the pad on her person, and destroys the used keys, although keeping a one time pad on your person seems somewhat foolish!

The commercial and industrial use of cryptography since WW2 introduced a major problem. Commercial organisations need to exchange secure communications; the only way of exchanging keys seemed to be by using trusted couriers. The amount of courier traffic began to grow out of control. It was the invention of public key cryptography that solved the key distribution problem.

The idea itself is relatively simple! Alice and Bob wish to communicate by post, but they know that Eve has infiltrated the postal service, and any letter they send will be opened and read unless it is securely "sealed".

Alice can put a letter in a chest, padlock the chest, and send it to Bob; but Bob will be unable to open the chest unless he already has a copy of Alice's key!

The solution is such:

Alice puts her letter in the chest, padlocks it and sends it to Bob. Now Bob cannot open the chest. Instead, he puts his own padlock on the chest and sends it back to Alice. Now Alice removes her padlock and returns the chest to Bob, who then simply has to remove his own padlock and open the chest! Extrapolating this to the reality of secure internet traffic and online banking is perhaps not so trivial.

To formalise the concept:

Let:

Alice's encryption and decryption functions be e_A and d_A and let Bob's be e_B and d_B .

This means that Alice encrypts the plaintext, p, as $e_A(p)$.

She can also decrypt this to p, which means that

$$d_A(e_A(p)) = p.$$

Alice wants to send a message to Bob using the above method.

She must first encrypt the plaintext message, p, as: $e_A(p)$

Then send it to Bob.

He encrypts it as $e_B(e_A(p))$ and returns it to Alice.

Now we have to make a crucial assumption:

e_A and e_B must commute, that is,

$$e_A \circ e_B = e_B \circ e_A \,.$$

This is the equivalent of Bob applying a padlock to Alice's padlock!

Now Alice has $(e_B \circ e_A)(p)$, which is equal to $e_A \circ e_B (p) = e_A(e_B(p))$ according to our assumption. Alice can now decrypt this to give $d_A(e_A(e_B(p))) = e_B(p)$ and send this to Bob, who then calculates $d_B(e_B(p)) = p$.

At no time during the transaction is any unencrypted message transmitted or any key exchanged. Note that the operations of putting two padlocks onto a chest do indeed commute! The method would not work if, instead, Bob put the chest inside another chest and locked the outer chest; the operations don't commute in this case!

If the letter that Alice sends to Bob is the key to a cipher (ideally a one-time pad), then Alice and Bob can now use this cipher in the usual way to communicate safely, without the need for the back and forth originally required. The system only depends on the security of the ciphers used by Alice and Bob for the exchange, and the fact that they must commute.

Now if Alice and Bob use **binary** (meaning only involving 0's and 1's. 1+1 = 0, 0+0 = 0, 0+1 = 1) one time pads for the key exchange, then these conditions are satisfied, since binary addition is a commutative operation.

However, further thought shows that this is not a solution at all! Suppose that Alice wants to send the string 1 securely to Bob (perhaps for later use as a one time pad).

She encrypts it as $1 \oplus k_A$, where k_A is a random key chosen by Alice and known to nobody else. Bob re encrypts this as $(1 \oplus k_A) \oplus k_B$, where k_B is a random key chosen by Bob and known to nobody else. Now $(1 \oplus k_A) \oplus k_B = (1 \oplus k_B) \oplus k_A$, so when Alice re encrypts this message with k_A she obtains:

$$((1 \oplus k_B) \oplus k_A) \oplus k_A = (1 \oplus k_B) \oplus (k_A \oplus k_A) = 1 \oplus k_B$$

and when Bob finally re-encrypts this with k B he obtains

$$(1 \oplus k_B) \oplus k_B = 1.$$

This is the exact analogue of the chest with two keys. If Eve only intercepts one of these three transmissions, it is impossible for her to read the message, since each is securely encrypted with a one-time pad. However, we must assume that Eve will intercept all three transmissions. Now if she simply adds all three together mod 2, she obtains

$$(1 \oplus k_A) \oplus (1 \oplus k_A \oplus k_B) \oplus (1 \oplus k_B) = 1$$

and she has the message!

Diffie and Hellman tackled this problem and came up with an ingenious and radical solution. They discovered that it is not even necessary to share the keys at all! The reason for the insecurity of the above protocol is that decryption is just as simple as encryption for someone who possesses the key; for binary addition, it is exactly the same operation. A cipher with this property is called symmetric. The trick is to construct an asymmetric cipher, where decryption is disastrously difficult even if you are in possession of the key. For us to understand this we must study when something is "easy" or "difficult". Mathematicians know this as Complexity Theory.

First we must understand the size of a problem. It is the number of "blocks" needed to write down the input data. (It doesn't matter if we decide to use only the binary alphabet, and define the size of a problem instance to be the number of bits of input data. If for example, we write the number N in base 2 instead of base 10, we need only $\log_2(10) = 2.30\ldots$ times as many blocks ; a constant factor does not matter here.

We now briefly look at complexity classes:

1. A problem lies in P, or is polynomial-time solvable, if there is an algorithm which can solve an instance of the problem of size n in at most p(n) for some polynomial p.

2. A problem lies in NP, or is non-deterministic polynomial-time solvable, if there is an algorithm which can check the correctness of a proposed solution of a problem instance of size n in at most p(n) steps, for some polynomial p.

3. A problem lies in PSpace, or is polynomial-space solvable, if there is an algorithm which can solve an instance of the problem of size n using at most p(n) steps, for some polynomial p.

4. A problem lies in ExpTime, or is exponential-time solvable, if there is an algorithm which can solve an instance of the problem in at most $2^{p(n)}$ steps,

for some polynomial p.

A problem of higher complexity is harder. If a problem takes n^3 steps to solve, and each step takes a nanosecond, then an instance of size 1000 can be solved in a second, and an instance of size 10000 in 3 months. However, if it takes 2^n steps, then we can solve an instance of size 30 in a second, while an instance of size 100 will take longer than the age of the universe!

Generally, polynomial-time problems are easy, while exponential time problems are hard:

$$P \subseteq NP \subseteq PSpace \subseteq ExpTime$$

9 PUBLIC-KEY CRYPTOGRAPHY

The idea of public key cryptography based on (complexity of problems) the fact that there are easy and hard problems was devised by Diffie and Hellman in the 1970s. This is one of the great ideas of the last century!

Some terminology that is often used here is that of 'one-way functions'. A function $f: A \to B$ is said to be one way if it is easy to compute, f, but hard to compute the inverse function from B to A. It is a trapdoor one way function if there is a piece of information which makes the computation of the inverse function easy.

So, for public key cryptography, we want encryption to be a trapdoor one way function, where the

key to the trapdoor is the secret key. The function from secret key to public key should be a one way function.

The RSA Cryptosystem

The system depends on the following problems. (It is mainly based on the difficulty in finding the prime factors of large numbers!)

The easy problems below are all in P. It is not known

whether the hard problems are NP-complete.

Easy problems

1. Test whether an integer N is prime.

2. Given a and n, find gcd(a, n) and (if it is 1) find an inverse of a mod n.

3. Calculate the transformation T e : x → x e mod N.

Hard problems

4. Given an integer N, factorise it into its prime factors.

5. Given an integer N, calculate $\lambda(N)$ (or $\varphi(N)$).

6. Given N and e, find d such that T_d is the inverse of T_e mod N.

Problem 1: Note that division does not solve this problem efficiently. For a number N requiring n bits of input is one which has n digits when written in base 2, and hence is of size roughly 2^n ; its square root is about $2^{n/2}$, and trial division would require about half this many steps.

Problem 2: This is solved by Euclid's algorithm, as shown previously.

Problem 3: This problem seems hard, for two reasons:

- The number x e will be absolutely vast, with about e log x digits (recall that the number of digits of e is part of the size of the input; if e has 100 digits, then x^e has too many digits to write down. The number is greater than the number of atoms in the universe!

- We have to perform $e - 1$ multiplications to find x^e = $x \cdot x \cdot x \cdots x$ e factors.

We can deal with the first obstacle by doing all calculations in mod n. So to calculate *ab* mod n, (where a,b < n), we first calculate *ab* as an integer, then take the remainder on division by *n.* In this way we never have to deal with a number larger than n^2 during the calculation.

The second obstacle is overcome by writing *e* in base e: $2^{a_1} + 2^{a_2} + ... + 2^{a_k}$. By $a_1 - 1$ successive squarings, calculate x_2 , $x 2^2$, . . . , $x_2^{a_1}$. Now x^e can be obtained by k − 1 further multiplications.

Problems 4 - 6 are not known to be NP-complete, so it is possible that they may not be as hard as we consider them to be. However, centuries of work by mathematicians has failed to discover an 'easy' algorithm to factorise large numbers. (The advent of quantum computation would change this!)

We will be concerned only with numbers N which are the product of two distinct primes p and q. So we really need the special case of 4 which asks:

Given a number N which is known to be the product of two distinct prime factors, find the factors.

Even this problem is currently unyielding.

But we do know that if it is known that N is the product of two distinct primes, then problems 4 and 5 are equivalent, in the sense that knowledge of a solution of one would enable us to solve the other.

Theorem: Let N be the product of two distinct primes. Then, from any one of the following, we can compute the others in a polynomial number of steps:

- the prime factors of N

- $\varphi(N)$

- $\lambda(N)$

Carmichael's lambda-function $\lambda(n)$ is defined to be the smallest number, *m*, such that $a^m \equiv 1$ (mod n) for all *a* such that gcd(a, n) = 1. For example, $\varphi(35) = 24$ but $\lambda(35) = 12$

Practical Implementation:

Bob chooses two large prime numbers p_B and q_B, assumed to be random. Knowing p_B and q_B , Bob computes their product $N_B = p_B q_B$. He can also compute $\lambda(N_B) = \text{lcm}(p_B - 1, q_B - 1)$. He now calculated a large 'exponent' e_B satisfying $\gcd(e_B, \lambda(N_B)) = 1$, by the use of Euclid's Algorithm. This also gives the inverse of e_B mod $\lambda(N_B)$, that is the number such that T_{dB} is the inverse of T_{eB} , where $T_{eB} : x \rightarrow x^{e_B}$ (mod N_B).

Bob publishes N_B and e_B , and keeps the factorisation of N_B and the number d_B secret. If Alice wishes to send a message to Bob, she first transforms her message into a number x less than N_B .

Now she computes $z = T_{eB}(x)$ and sends this to Bob. Bob deciphers the message by applying the inverse function

T_{dB} to it. This gives a number less than N_B and congruent to x (mod N_B). Since x is also less than N_B, the resulting decryption is correct. If Eve intercepts the message z, she has to compute $T_{dB}(z)$, which is a hard problem (problem 6 above). Alternatively, she could compute d_B from the published value of e_B. Since d_B is the inverse of e_B mod $\lambda(N_B)$, this requires her to calculate $\lambda(N_B)$, which is also hard (problem 5). Finally, she could try to factorise N_B, this too, is hard (problem 4). So the cipher is secure!!

Finally, back to Diffie and Hellman:

Alice wants to send a secret message to Bob. Alice and Bob agree on a modulus p, where p is a prime number. They must share the prime p, so they assume that Eve can get hold of it! Each of them chooses a number coprime to $\lambda(p) = p - 1$, and computes its inverse. These numbers are not revealed. Alice chooses d_A and e_A, Bob chooses d_B and e_B. Note that the commutation condition still holds:

$$T_{dA}\,T_{dB}(x) = x^{d_A d_B} \bmod p = T_{dB}T_{dA}(x)$$

Alice takes the message x and applies T_{eA}. She sends $T_{eA}(x)$ to Bob.

Bob applies T_{eB} and returns $T_{eB}T_{eA}(x)$ to Alice.

Alice applies T_{dA} and returns

$$T_{dA}T_{eB}T_{eA}(x) = T_{dA}T_{eA}T_{eB}(x) = T_{eB}(x) \text{ to Bob.}$$

Bob then applies applies T_{dB} and recovers

$$T_{dB}T_{eB}(x) = x, \text{ the original message!}$$

There is currently no known weakness in this method, so even if Eve intercepts all the messages that pass between Alice and Bob, she cannot discover x, even if she knows the modulus *p.*

Digital Signatures:

There is a serious potential weakness of public-key cryptography. Eve cannot read Alice's message to Bob. But, since Bob's key is public, Eve can write her own message to Bob purporting to come from Alice, encrypt it with Bob's key, and substitute it for Alice's authentic message on the communication channel!

The solution to this problem is very interesting. Firstly, it involves Alice **decrypting** the plaintext message using **her own key**. The result is complete and utter nonsense! She then adds a preamble in plaintext stating something along the lines of *"This is a confirmed signed message from Alice".* She then encrypts the whole thing using Bob's public key and sends it to Bob. Bob now decrypts the whole thing: he will see some nonsense and the statement *"This is a confirmed signed message from Alice",* he will then proceed to **encrypt** the nonsense using Alice's public key. Bob now has the message Alice intended only for him!!

Hopefully, this has been an interesting introduction to the world of modern cryptography. There are still major leaps and developments to be made in this rapidly growing and expanding field.

An idea that is of particular interest to me is that of understanding which other mathematically "hard" problems can be used to develop a crypto system.

A particular example is adapting the "P" hard problem of "counting perfect matchings" or "counting complete transversals*" of graphs (with a large number of- maybe prime- vertices) to public key cryptography. This is a problem that combines Graph Theory, Combinatorics and Cryptography!

Further topics that are a must to read up on are Elliptic Curve Cryptography and Quantum Computing.

*Note: Complete Transversal = Set of Disjoint edges (no shared endpoints) which *span* the graph (all vertices included). Generally, it is "easy" to find perfect matchings, but "hard" to *count* how many!

ABOUT THE AUTHOR

Mustafa Zia is a Mathematics graduate with a zeal for all things technical, functional and tech-related.

His passions include bodybuilding, tinkering with electronics and restoring classic cars.